Self-Discipline

Conquer Laziness & Procrastination & Start Achieving Your Goals Today

Harrison Parker

©Copyright 2020 by Cascade Publishing

All rights reserved.

It is not legal to reproduce, duplicate, or transmit any part of this document in either electronic means or in printed format. Recording of this publication is strictly prohibited.

TABLE OF CONTENTS

Introduction: 1

Chapter One: The Basics Of Self-Discipline 3

Chapter Two: Discipline Killing Habits 12

Chapter Three: Self-Discipline Friendly Environment . 16

Chapter Four: The Power Of Goals And Journaling 20

Chapter Five: The Two Minute Rule 28

Chapter Six: Mindset Hacking 34

Chapter Seven: Healthy Habits For Discipline 37

Chapter Eight: Navy Seals To The Rescue 41

Chapter Nine: Popular Self-Discipline Tactics 45

Conclusion 52

Introduction

Staying focused at the task at hand can be difficult for many people, with various distractions impeding their progress. Add in the fact that many tasks that we must accomplish can appear 'boring' or just something we lack the inspiration to complete, and we have a recipe for disaster.

It's not a matter of being lazy or not. It's a matter of having the appropriate tools to keep yourself disciplined enough to focus on what you need to do, and simply getting it done. Anybody can learn how to be disciplined, and in turn start accomplishing everything they desire with a few simple steps. In the forthcoming chapters, we will explore what it means to have self-discipline, as well as ways to cultivate self-discipline.

There is a good chance that at some point in your life somebody has told you that you need to stop being lazy or that you lack willpower. Those words likely did nothing more than make you feel worse about yourself, and that's all those words will ever do. Belittling someone has never helped a person change, nor are those words very truthful.

A lack of self-discipline is not the act of laziness. It's an act of the mind. If you learn how to fine tune your mind, and rewire the way you think, you can do away with the lack of focus that many suffer from. Sure, willpower plays a part in your self-discipline, but you don't have to feel as if you are forcing yourself to do things.

The good news is, there are countless techniques to overcome these issues, and even numerous tools that the Navy Seals implement to improve their self-discipline. There is also a two-minute rule that will help to subdue that procrastination.

Instead of wasting any more time, let's jump right into learning more about self-discipline.

Chapter One:

The Basics of Self-Discipline

Most of my failures had been attributed to my own weaknesses like quitting, taking the easy way out, and procrastination. All of these I found out, were signs of not having self-discipline.

Upon further reflection, my successes had many opposing strategies. They had all been the result of self-discipline. I realized that my greatest triumphs had transpired when I constantly applied myself, doing whatever I had to, whether I wanted to or not.

I knew that if I wanted to succeed, this was something I had to explore further. I was tired of feeling like a loser. I was tired of always living below my capabilities and selling myself short.

I finally decided to put my feelings aside and started working on myself. I was a full-time student for seven years, while working in endless jobs to pay for my education.

Slowly but surely I transformed my body from being overweight to a now happier, healthier and fitter version of myself. All of this didn't happen overnight. However, I couldn't have done any of this if I didn't maintain the proper self-discipline.

There were days when it was uncomfortable and others that were brutally tough, but I knew I had to keep pushing. I would never have forgiven myself if I hadn't seen it through. I knew it would be something I would regret for the rest of my life. Although my desires were strong, the path I was walking wasn't ever easy.

I worked long hours and never saw any immediate rewards. I pushed my body until I wanted to puke. The next day it was hard to even walk to the bathroom because I was so sore.

I studied endlessly for every exam, while failing at many business ventures. I didn't ever look for admiration or sympathy. I was on my own journey, and it was what it was.

I feel privileged that I partook in these opportunities. Likewise, I will be forever grateful for the failures that shaped my life. And although I was frustrated for majority of the time, I knew deep down that it would all be worth it in the end. Quitting eventually never became an option for me, as staying in the same position a year from now, 5 years from now, 10 years from now, quite honestly frightened the hell out of me.

One thing that was worse than struggling with my self-discipline, was serving it with a huge dollop of self-blame and anger directed at myself. I faced days where all I could think about was:

- "What is wrong with me?"
- "Why can't I focus?"
- "Why is it taking me so long to finish this simple task?"
- "Why did I not go to the gym?"
- "Why am I so easily distracted?"
- "Why can't I stop procrastinating?"
- "Why did I eat that sixth piece of pizza?"
- "How can I rid of this brain fog?"
- "Am I depressed?"

- "Is this really worth it?"

What I had to remember was that we humans aren't born with a natural ability to control and regulate ourselves. These are skills that our youthful brains develop and cultivate when we receive the correct emotional attention from our parents during our upbringing.

What Exactly is Self-Discipline?

Self-Discipline is the ability to resist instant gratification, in favor of greater gain or more substantial rewards. It is doing the things that you know you have to do, even if you don't feel like it. It is persevering, even when it feels uncomfortable. It is pushing through any and all obstacles in your way.

Every form of self-discipline can be categorized into two groupings. Those who take action, and those whose don't.

Once you embrace self-discipline, you will have more control over yourself and the life you live. Building a strong sense of self-discipline is easy once you have a good reason for doing so. Having a large "why" will keep you on the right track toward your ultimate goal. We will look into this later on.

Characteristics of the Self-Disciplined

- Driven by Passion

Anyone who can apply self-discipline to their goals will be excited about everything they do. Their passions fuel them with all the motivation they need to work through all of the monotony. How can you maintain self-discipline when you don't have any interest in the outcome? It's simple, you have to do things that matter to you.

- Long Term Vision

These individuals understand that true success will take time, and it isn't going to happen overnight. The end goal is so important, that they will persist through any struggles until they have accomplished or received all that they desire. There is no temptation to quit, even if their objective has not manifested within a couple of days, weeks, months or even years.

- Necessary Sacrifices

If there is somebody or something that is distracting them from their objective/goals, they will not hesitate to remove that toxicity. This can be a hard trigger to pull, but you will soon realize that you are serious about achieving your goals when you are willing to sacrifice other things to attain to them.

- Do Not Fear Hard Work

People with high levels of self-discipline flourish in the presence of adversity. It is juvenile to think that things will come easy. For all the things that challenge you will gift you with the greatest reward. Self-disciplined individuals understand that it is in their best interest to tackle every obstacle head-on. They thoroughly enjoy a challenge and thrive off hard work.

- Take Action

Individuals that embody self-discipline won't waste any time waiting and wishing for things to appear. They just won't wait. They find a favorable strategy and begin taking action. The only obstacle in the way at this point is yourself. You will never know, if you never try.

How Important is Self-Discipline?

If you don't have self-discipline, sadly, you are not going to get very far in life. You aren't going to stick with anything long enough to see it come to fruition. The larger your goals, the more discipline you require. The crazy thing is, you don't even need to be the most intelligent or talented person, you just have to put in the work. If you have set clear goals and push through any adversities, nothing can stop you.

How to Gain More Self-Discipline?

- Understand Your Weaknesses

You have to identify your weaknesses, and realize the areas that you can improve on. Observe your current routines and patterns and isolate those weaknesses. Look for areas in your life where you lack discipline and identify how you can improve those flaws.

- Dispose of the Option to Quit

Never give yourself permission to quit. When you decide to do something, keep persisting until it is done. Change your strategy if you need to, but quitting should never be considered. Failure is simply the opportunity to begin again, this time more intelligently.

- Set Your Goals and Execute a Strategy

Maintaining your discipline is easy when you know what you want, why you want it, and have a clear pathway figured out. Disregard as much conscious thought as you can. Figure out what it is you want and set goals in place. Create methods to achieve those aspirations and then begin to execute your plan. Take action and make any necessary changes as you go. Nothing will ever go exactly to plan, so take each day as it comes and conquer every obstacle along the way.

- Create Habits That Empower You

You absolutely MUST create habits that will empower you. They have to be in line with what you want and who you want to be. Dispose of anything that doesn't serve you. Being passionate about your daily routine drastically improves the consistency and likelihood of success. If you don't like reading, try audiobooks. If you don't enjoy running, try cycling. If you work more efficiently in the afternoon, forego the morning work and focus your attention on other developing other habits in the morning.

- KISS

Keep it simple stupid. It doesn't have to be complicated, so don't make it complicated. It isn't necessary. Never waste your energy or time trying to sound smart or look good. Invest your energy and time into getting things done the easiest way you can.

- Eat Healthy

A wholesome and nutritious diet can fuel your body and mind with a prolonged energy source that allows you to reinvest yourself into your important goals. People who consume a healthy diet will be physically and mentally stronger than those who consume unhealthy eating habits. Living a healthy life will keep you disciplined and focused when you need it the most. I found that healthy eating attributed to a lot of my productivity. It provided me with a solid foundation to build my day upon.

- Don't Force Yourself Out of the Game

Never make your goals so important that you force yourself out of the game. You should rather focus on the process or "the chase". Refine and improve on the process, create a more efficient system that works in your favor and you will prevail. There are people out there who have accomplished everything that you are trying to achieve. They have it all, so why can't you? You just have to apply yourself and take action.

- You Need to Reinvent Yourself

You have to visualize yourself as a person who is highly motivated and self-disciplined. Your past experiences of quitting don't matter anymore, so use this to your advantage. You know how it feels to quit, you know where it leaves you. Shift your perspective, change your daily routines, eat healthier, plan ahead, it really is quite simple in theory. The hard part is taking action! A great practice is to model your behaviors off someone in a position you aspire to be. If you want to run a marathon for example, the best way to accomplish this objective would be to practice similar habits to that of a marathon runner.

- Have Fun

Many of the tasks that you may have to complete in order to reach your goals are going to be monotonous or boring. There are also going to be times that you need to harness more self-discipline than others. It isn't always going to be fun, but attempt to make it as fun as you possibly can. Once you enjoy what you are doing, you tend to stick with it, do it more often, and bring you closer to reaching your goals.

Discipline Can Improve Your Quality of Life

- You Could Experience Better Health

Everyone wishes for improved health and well-being. You know what you need to do. You have to move your body. You have to burn more calories than you eat. You need to build up strength. You need to eat cleaner. Stop putting toxins in your body. This is going to take some self-discipline and self-control especially when you are just starting this journey. If you value your life and love yourself, is there another way to live?

- You Can Have More Money

Being wealthy isn't complicated. You simply have to make sure you spend less than you earn. You need discipline so you can stick to a budget. You need to develop the willpower, so you don't spend money on things that you don't need. If you are already in debt, it is going to take more discipline to be able to pay off your bills each month and stop spending your money on other materialistic objects. Figure out what your ideal finances will look like, create a plan, and stick with it. Decide whether you desire more money, or the freedom it enables.

- Learn New Skills

Learning any new skill is going to require repetition and the discipline to keep showing up. Regardless of whether it is a new language, a new hobby, or an instrument, all of the principles remain the same. Once the excitement wears off, all you will be left with is your determination to reach your objective. In other words, your success depends on how much you really want it. How meaningful are your future goals in life? Are you happy with being mediocre? How much are you willing to sacrifice? This is your answer. It is completely okay to be content with less, but understanding where you stand is an important process of knowing what you need to do.

Seven Benefits of Self-Discipline

- Boosted Self Esteem and Pride

If you are able to set worthy goals and stick to it long enough to accomplish them, your self-esteem will go through the roof. You will enjoy reaping the rewards along the way and take pride in all things you do. Your confidence levels will skyrocket as you adapt to new changes, and you will radiate happiness form within.

- Staying Away From What Hurts You

You need to have enough self-discipline to stay away from everything that could destroy you including substances, circumstances, and or people. Being successful in life is as much about knowing when to say "yes" and when to say "no." Self-discipline lets you stay away from all those self-defeating actions and choices.

- Increases Your Success Rate

Self-discipline is extremely important when it comes to all aspects of life. Why? Well, there are many distractions that can push you off course. You have to stand strong. You have to be willing to say "no" to some things, and "yes" to contributions that will make a difference. Keep refining and learning as you go. The longer you can hang in there, your chances of success increase drastically. There isn't anything mysterious or magical about it.

- Healthier Body and Mind

With increased levels of exercise in conjunction with healthy eating you will drastically improve mental clarity, feel stronger, look healthier, and your positive experiences will intensify. Do I need to say anything else? The hard part is the beginning. The first few days, weeks, or months might really blow. However, you aren't going to quit because you aren't a quitter. You are a winner. You have the willpower to set goals and take any action needed until you reach those goals. In spite of all the temptations to quit, you will stay on course until you have reached your destination.

- Remove Any Competition

This world we live in is highly competitive. This isn't to say that you have to be aggressive, and you have to crush everybody around you. Whatever it is you want, other people may want the same things. When you slack off, there will be someone who is working harder to get what you want. It boils down to the person who has the most self-discipline. Many people are just lazy, and they don't want to do anything that they don't have to, don't be that guy. Go the extra mile.

- Inspire Others

Anytime you apply self-discipline and start seeing results, you will undoubtedly inspire others around you. These people feel encouraged to raise their standards to match your energy. It is a wonderful thing when somebody thanks you for being an inspiration especially when it may have been completely unintentional on your behalf. Nevertheless, use this gratitude as motivation to build bigger and greater things while inspiring more people around you.

- Living Your Best Life

The best benefit of self-discipline is it allows you to live life on your terms. You will achieve all of the goals that mean something to you. You will be able to make all the choices and decisions that will benefit you. Self-discipline is your crown jewel when it comes to achievements and personal growth. Once you are able to harness all the power of your self-discipline, the world will open up for you. You will be your best self. You will be living your best life. And to be honest, you don't deserve anything less than that.

Chapter Two:

Discipline Killing Habits

There is a good chance that your lack of discipline has been instigated by many of your daily habits. Habits are behaviors formed through repetition, with each passing day becoming more automatic or consistent. Unfortunately, not all of these behaviors develop into good practices. Most people will have developed several bad habits over time that they would love to kick, and this is completely normal. However, we are going to discuss various bad habits that are killing your self-discipline in particular. Whether you familiarize with one or all of these habits, don't be alarmed. It doesn't make you a bad person, just a victim of circumstance. The good news is, you can break all of these habits.

Non-Stop Snacking

Overeating and non-stop snacking is a common concern amongst many people. When you lose touch with your body's natural satisfaction and hunger indicators, it can lead to chronic overeating. This behavior will likely cause you to gain unhealthy weight, which can lead to heart disease, diabetes, and other severe health complications. If you enjoy snacking on junk food, the unfortunate side-effect is that you are also inundating your body with terrible nutrition. The fact that you have lost control over your eating is why this habit damages your discipline levels.

With determination, anybody can overcome their bad eating habits, and reach a healthier weight. When you start to pay attention to your hunger signals and change your snacks to healthy alternatives, you will discourage energy slumps, lose weight, control cravings, and boost your overall well-being. You will also drastically minimize the intake of harmful nutrients like processed sugars and trans fats.

Wasting Time with Social Media

The more time spent indulging in social media, the less physically active you become, the more prone to distraction and procrastination. There is a good chance that this wasted time is consuming the time that you would otherwise be using to improve yourself as a human being.

When you limit your time spent on social media platforms, you inherently increase the amount of time to partake in other activities. These activities can range from increased exercise, learning new skills, working more efficiently. In turn, you gain boosted energy levels, newly acquired talents, and a better workflow depending on which activities you supplement during this time. You will also find that you gain boosted energy levels, an improved quality of sleep, and a sharper mind to name a few additional benefits. In conjunction, you will improve your self-confidence and self-discipline exponentially.

Overspending

Financial stress and anxiety can contribute to many negative downfalls including gaining or losing weight, excessive drinking or smoking, ulcers, panic attacks, pains and aches, digestive difficulties, headaches, insomnia, depression, and high blood pressure.

I get it, it's hard, but getting out of debt works a lot like losing weight. It will take time, and it will be tough on your lifestyle and ego. You will have to remain vigilant, and learn to not fall back to your old spending habits. Those who succeed and many do, the results are remarkable. You will feel as if you have more control over your life with fewer concerns and less stress. You'll have fewer headaches, stop overeating, and sleep better. Find ways to cut your spending and focus on the joys of life and improve relationships.

Consuming Too Much Fast Food

Consuming a diet of cheeseburgers and fries washed down with milkshakes and soda will initiate a bigger waistline and possibly many other concerning factors, like diabetes and heart disease. Foods high in trans-fat cause an increase in bad cholesterol, contributing to the hardening of your arteries.

Making the switch to healthier foods has substantial and immediate benefits. An everlasting lifestyle change is not going to be easy. Fast food is convenient, inexpensive, and let's be honest, delicious. Healthy eating is going to take more time and thought, but it is worth it. Besides losing some weight and slimming down, you also protect yourself from health problems, regain improved energy levels, and simply feel better. You can save money if you make your own meals instead of eating out. Meal prepping is a great exercise to enact into your routine, having meals readily available to reheat when required eliminates any stresses or time constraints.

Acting In Ways That Leave you Stressed, Angry, or Worried

Partaking in an unhealthy lifestyle will lead to a cascade of stress hormones that will increase your blood sugar and blood pressure, slow your digestion, lower your immunity, and make you feel unpleasant. Nature only meant for stress to be a short-lived response when faced with an incoming threat, but within our modern lives, many often develop chronic stress. This stress has far-reaching impacts on your health, and cause you to overeat. All of this comes together in a horrible cocktail that can cause diabetes, heart disease, and other problems.

Through stress-reduction techniques, you can protect your heart, lower blood sugar, ease chronic pain, reduce depression, improve immunity, and lower your blood sugar. Having a new sense of joy and control is better than anything, and the physical benefits are abundant.

Drinking Too Much Alcohol

You might not like to hear it, but the fact of the matter is alcohol is poison to the body, and when you over-drink, it can have disastrous effects. Men who regularly drink three or more alcoholic beverages a day, and women who drink two or more, are at a greater risk of liver damage, depression, high blood pressure, and various forms of cancer. Women tend to be more sensitive to alcohol and can further develop memory loss, brittle bones, and heart disease.

Not long after you quit drinking or cut back, you will find that your digestion will improve and you will sleep better. Your blood sugar will also reach normal levels and remain steady. You will have an overall healthier body and cardiovascular system. Besides feeling more energetic, you will build superior relationships and welcome a better life.

Smoking

When it comes to encumbering your health, there aren't many habits that are as harmful as smoking cigarettes. It is the direct cause of 30% of all heart disease deaths, 30% of cancer deaths, and 80 to 90% of all lung cancer deaths. It also increases your likelihood of contracting bladder, throat, and mouth cancer. Likewise, smoking astronomically raises your chances of high blood pressure, strokes, and heart attacks, on top of aggravating or triggering respiratory issues like asthma and bronchitis.

The health benefits of breaking your smoking habit are almost immediate with the cardiovascular system and lungs starting to mend within minutes. After a month of not smoking, the lungs will perform more efficiently, you will cough less, gain more energy, and not experience shortness of breath. It also reduces your chance of heart disease and cancer, gives you better endurance, and improves your sense of smell and taste. You also won't reek of cigarettes anymore, and that will boost your confidence.

All of these habits have one thing in common, they prevent you from doing the things you should be doing. Whether you lack the energy to do things because of the food you eat or if you have to repeatedly step out for a smoke, these are some habits that will prevent you from achieving your goals. Of course there are many more, however, by now I'm sure you get the point.

Chapter Three:

Self-Discipline Friendly Environment

The best way to maintain discipline is to create an environment conducive for discipline. Setting up a self-discipline friendly environment can help you in countless areas of your life, such as school, work, and home. Let's take a look at the best ways to improve your environment.

Get Rid of Distractions

When you are looking to build your self-discipline, you first need to isolate any distractions in your life. When you can identify those disturbances you will be able to begin the process of elimination.

One common distraction for most of us is our smartphone. We can easily get caught up in messaging friends during the day or scrolling through our social media in order to find out what our friends are up to. It is vital that you limit these distractions when building self-discipline, as they will consume your willpower, energy and time.

A great practice is to switch your smartphone onto airplane or do not disturb mode. Alternatively, smartphones now have features built in that allow you to set limitations on all or individual applications. This is an outstanding feature that allows you to limit certain apps to specific times of the day, or limit the amount of time per day an app can be utilized. Defining these boundaries really allows you to hone in on the tasks that need to be completed before you enjoy the likes of social media. The idea is to create an environment that cultivates focus on the task at hand.

Know Your Inclinations

Understanding your inclinations means that you recognize your uniqueness and needs. Your need could be that you tend to get hungry at certain times during the day, or you may have a unique inclination towards certain times of the day where you have an increase in energy.

It is important to identify these inclinations, and start utilizing them in your favor. For example, if you know that you are more energized during the afternoon, schedule your most challenging task for that time of day. This means you won't use up as much mental energy to work on it.

Have A Reward Waiting

Developing your self-discipline has a strong connection to your motivation levels. Maintaining high levels of motivation will make it a lot easier for you to remain focused and disciplined on what you need to do.

To assist in this process, have a reward system set up for yourself once you finish your task. This could be as simple as taking a break upon completion, or after an allocated time period. The opportunity to briefly unwind from the task at hand will help to recharge your mind and encourage an energy boost. While this may seem like a small step, when you practice this often, you will be able to build up your drive that will lead to more self-discipline.

Have Your Schedule Posted

We will talk about making goals in the next chapter, but once you have identified your goals and broken them down into smaller processes, you need to apply them to your schedule. The best way to make sure you don't forget your schedule is to post in a place where you will see it, regularly.

You can keep your schedule in an app on your phone or computer, but it highly recommended to also have a paper version handy. This way, you don't run the risk of getting distracted by your phone when you go to check what you need to do. Plus, simply looking up at your wall and seeing the list of things you need to do right in front of you is a bit of a motivational boost.

Use Technology Wisely

While technology can most definitely be a distraction, it can also be extremely useful. You can use technology to create reminders to help you remain disciplined. For instance, you can set yourself a timer for casual web browsing so that you don't spend all of your time browsing. This will make sure that you don't forget about your important tasks. As previously mentioned, smartphones can also monitor and limit your usage in certain categories including socials, entertainment, productivity and games.

Make Decisions Early

It's a great idea to start making decisions in advance to remove any other temptations. This means that you won't be as likely to procrastinate on doing what needs to be done. Scheduling and prioritize your important tasks the night before, and stay true to that plan.

Don't compromise when it comes to making decisions. After you have made a decision about something, you need to make sure that you follow through. Do your best not to end up changing your mind when you need to do something. When you do this, you will more likely to finish your task, and you will find that temptations are less likely to sway you.

Devise A Routine

One of the most effective ways to stay disciplined is to create a routine. A routine will help you to stay consistent with your daily tasks. After you have internalized your routine, it will become effortless, and you won't have to actively remind yourself of what to do. Consistency is the key here.

Your goal of having a routine is to make sure that you stay self-disciplined so that you will reach your goals. That means you have to come up with a routine that is going to maximize the work you do on a consistent basis.

Think about the type of routine you would like to establish to help with your discipline. The most important thing is to make sure that you have a realistic routine. This will ensure that you will actually follow it long term. This is crucial for staying disciplined, especially if a task is particularly difficult.

You can keep the routine realistic by remaining focused on tiny steps to start off with to find the momentum you need to work towards your goal. You can always adapt this routine and add to it if needed.

Once Again

The most important thing about creating a space that is conducive for self-discipline is that you stay consistent. If you minimize all possible distractions, phone, TV, and you have your schedule within reach, you can remain disciplined.

Also, make sure that you don't create unrealistic expectations for yourself. You can't expect to be perfect the first day you try out your new schedule. You're going to get the itch to check your phone, and you might scratch that itch, and that's fine. The important thing is to make sure, once you realize what you have done, that you correct the behavior and get back on track.

Continue working in this manner, and it will gradually become second nature. Stay consistent and don't beat yourself up in the process. It will take time, but it's absolutely doable.

Chapter Four:

The Power of Goals and Journaling

If you are looking for growth and productivity advice on the internet or in the self-help section of a bookstore or library, you will find an endless amount of information that will help you to improve your life.

However, don't allow yourself to be overwhelmed by everything you see. Will it help you? Most likely, yes. Can you implement it all at once? I'd say probably not. It's important that you remain vigilant on the basics and focus on creating healthier habits day by day.

Powerful Habits Called Keystone Habits

Keystone habits are behaviors that create a ripple effect in your life. Charles Duhigg explains in his book *The Power of Habit*: Keystone habits are "small changes or habits that people introduce into their routines that unintentionally carry over into other aspects of their lives."

Exercising regularly is a great example of a keystone habit. Through increased levels of activity you will create an influx of other positive effects. Your posture will improve. You will attract more self-confidence. You will feel more energized. Likewise, with exercise you will also eat healthier, further enhancing the benefits of improved health. You can see how this keeps continues right?

As with any habit, this takes a commitment to creating new habits, creating an environment to help you stick with your new habits, and then holding yourself accountable and taking action toward these new habits.

Well, where should you start? One habit that can easily be implemented and that has amazing potential to help transform your life is journaling.

What Exactly Is Journaling?

Journaling can be loosely defined as reflecting on certain emotions, activities or goals on a daily basis and writing down any thoughts or plans that come to mind. Since this is such a broad definition, it makes it a very versatile tool that can achieve various functions. You can journal on your computer, in a leather-bound journal, or even on a notepad.

- Your Creative Factory

Each night before you go to bed, use your journal to write down one problem that you wish to have solved. Contemplate this problem for a few moments, before proceeding to bed.

While you sleep, your subconscious mind goes to work to replay and reconsolidate your thoughts. Thomas Edison once said: "Never go to sleep without a request to your subconscious." Edison is implying that during slow wave sleep (SWS) you can direct your subconscious mind to creative thinking. It is during this phase of sleep that your subconscious can cultivate creative breakthroughs.

Once you wake up, grab for your journal as a type of "trap for your solutions." Try to tap into your thoughts that your subconscious presented to you during the night and write about anything that comes to mind. Write freely, and try not to discourage any thoughts. There will be time to reflect shortly.

In time, you may find that jotting interesting ideas down after waking up come more naturally, and develop overtime.

- A Dump For Your Thoughts

Journaling may also be a place where you dump all of your thoughts to just get them out of your head. You can do this at night, in the morning, or just anytime you need to clear your mind. You don't have to use journaling to solve your problems, but it may help to remove thoughts gain more mental clarity.

- Life's Compass

A journal is a great place to map out your priorities and values. You could allocate a specific time and just think about what really matters in your life. This helps you create a vision of how you would like your life unfold, and how you can break it down into smaller goals.

After you are clear about what you value and you have come up with a vision for your life, write everything down and revisit this page when you journal. Revisiting these thoughts can put everything into perspective and allows you to narrow your focus on the things that matter the most to you. This can sometimes give you the urgency you need to start working toward your goals and get you through your day.

- Setting Goals

Journaling is a very common method for setting goals. Similarly to the previous practice, you absolutely need to connect with your life's vision. You must know what you want, and set a connection between the present time and the destination.

With your end goal in focus, you want to work backwards toward the present. Break any of your long term goals down into smaller objectives or processes that you can accomplish daily, weekly or monthly. With each task you complete bringing you closer and closer to your long term goals.

What works for most people is scheduling a time to reevaluate your progress in different blocks. This means when you get to the end of one year, you make plans for the next year. When you get to the end of a month, you will set further goals for the next month. Once the week comes to an end, make plans for the following week. When you get to the end of your day, make plans for the next day. Find what works for you.

Coming up with a to-do list the day before is critical. You will be priming your subconscious for what is ahead of you, and it will make it easier to begin taking actions each morning when you know what you are supposed to do.

Break down your tasks into most important to least important, or fit them into your day in certain timeslots. Time blocking these tasks can keep you highly efficient and allow enhanced focus at the tasks at hand. I found that completing the more difficult tasks in the morning allowed me more energy for the rest of the day, less stress, and more time. Probably due to less procrastination and worrying.

- Accountability

Once your day is over, you need to check your journal and hold yourself accountable. You can create your own or use these questions to help you review your day:

- What did I accomplish today?
- What have I learnt today?
- Was I able to live up to my values and standards?
- What processes can I improve?
- What happened today that made me feel great?

Create a system that will help hold yourself accountable. There are many different approaches you can implement such as a daily reflective journaling session, rewarding yourself for completing certain tasks, or even gamifying accountability with your friends. Set up a group chat with like-minded individuals willing to commit to holding each other accountable. Have a weekly call, or progress reports that you can each post to prove to each other that you are putting in the work. If anyone is struggling, the group can inspire you to push through any adversities or laziness you may be facing. This can make sure that you never stop learning, feel obliged to work harder, and every passing day points you further in the right direction.

- Being Grateful

Being able to regularly express your gratitude is frequently overlooked in our daily lives because we have become so busy and occupied with other conducts.

You should try to keep this as part of your journaling habits, especially each night. Once you have looked over your day and have stayed accountable, try to write about three things you're grateful for. It might be something that happened that day or something small like eating your favorite foods at lunch, having a warm bed to crawl into, your health, or your family.

Writing down these thoughts at the end of your session while getting ready for bed, lets you get into a state of abundance, and you will end your day on a positive note.

Reflection is an Art

The common denominator throughout all of these techniques is the art of reflection. Why is this so effective and important? When you sit down each day and write in your journal, even if it is just for a few minutes, it will serve as a foundation for your thinking. It is a well-needed break where all your requests, noise, information gets shut off, and you have time to create and process.

This is a time that is reserved just for you. This is a time for you to reset yourself, gain some perspective and clarity. It allows you to calm down and regain some peace of mind.

Pain Plus Reflection Equals Progress

You might experience some pain or discomfort when you leave your comfort zone. You might face some resistance, fail, get rejected, have uncomfortable encounters, and ultimately not live up to your expectations. Reflection is when you learn something from that pain by processing, looking back at, and remaining accountable. Experience, evaluate, grow.

When to Journal

The Stoics idea of journaling looks something like this:

"In the morning, prepare for the day ahead and in the evening, but the day up for review."

You normally can't control everything that happens to you during your day, but whatever you do right after you wake up or right before you go to bed, seems to stick with you.

This is a great advantage to performing your evening and morning routines at the same time each day. Adding your journaling into these times can drastically help you adhere to your routine and allows you to reap all the benefits from it.

What Does a Session Look Like?

- Morning

The main reason behind journaling each morning is to shift into your best frame of mind, and to further prepare for the day ahead:

- Complete your thought dumping and creative factory routine. If you have problems coming up with anything, start with asking yourself how well you slept.

- Glance over your life vision, long-term goals, and values. Gain some motivation.

- Create a connection to the present, and commit to completing your most important tasks for the day.

- Evening

At the end of your day, right before you go to bed, your journaling sessions will help you become more aware of what you have learned during your day and how you can improve. It can help with holding yourself accountable, and stimulate your subconscious during sleep. You can also use this time to to wind down, let go, and end your day positively:

- Express what you are grateful for.
- Prime your subconscious with your main task or problem.
- Review your goals and create your to-do list for the next day.
- Visualize your long-term goals.
- Answer your accountability questions.

While journaling focus on your preferences and needs. If you are ever in doubt or overwhelmed, do less.

Quick tips:

The things you write down don't have to sound perfect. This is your journal. It doesn't matter if you read back over your entries or not. Never restrict your writing because of coherence, spelling, or grammar. If it is important to you, rewrite finalized ideas into a separate journal to keep it all neat. The main idea is to release thoughts. Worrying about grammar or spelling may hinder your ideas.

Your sessions don't have to be extensive. It only takes ten minutes for you to reap all the rewards of journaling.

Write less. You need to find a balance. You don't want to look at journaling as a burden. So, do what works for you, as there are no set rules to adhere to. You need to see it as a tool to liberate you, not a chore.

Call to Action

You can start journaling today by simply placing some paper and a pen on your bedside table. While you are getting ready for bed, write down some thoughts, and once you wake up do the same. See if this helps you get through your day.

With time, you can begin transitioning into a notebook and implementing it into your routine. If it were to become a habit that you implement for the rest of your life, and you decide to record the lessons that you have learned, it isn't just going to serve you but for generations to come. That is if you decide to pass it down.

Chapter Five:

The Two Minute Rule

I learned some time ago about one simple rule that helped put a halt to my procrastination. It also helped me take control of both my good and bad habits. The best part about this hack is that it is extremely easy to implement into your daily routine.

You can quit procrastinating by using the simple "two-minute rule." This rule makes it easier for you to begin things that you know you need to be doing, but would typically put off doing.

Most of the things that you need to do throughout your day aren't normally hard tasks. You have all the skills and talents you need to get them done. You just have a habit of avoiding them for various reasons.

This two-minute rule helps you overcome your laziness and procrastination by making it easier for you to begin taking action to the point where you just can't say no. This two-minute rule is broken down into two segments.

If You Can Do It In Under Two Minutes, Do It Right Now

It is very surprising how many tasks we actually don't do that we can get done in under two minutes. Here are some examples, sending an email, cleaning the benchtop, taking out the trash, putting the laundry in the washer, making your bed, etc.

If you have a task to do that you know will only take you two minutes or less, follow this rule and do it immediately. Tick it off the list and now you can forget about it.

When You Begin New Habits, It Needs To Take Less Than Two Minutes To Do It

Could all of your goals be completed in under two minutes? Of course not. But each task could be started in less than two minutes. This is the purpose behind the rule. It might sound like a strategy that is just too easy for your huge goals in life, but it isn't. This can work for any goal due to one reason: real-life physics.

Real-Life Physics

The two-minute rule works for large goals and smaller goals alike due to the inertia in life. Once you begin something, it becomes easier to involve yourself in the process. The two-minute rule is great since it embraces the idea that all kinds of opportunities can arise once you get started.

If you want to become a better writer, just write one paragraph, or sentence even. You might find that you strike gold and continue to write non-stop for an hour to cultivate an idea or concept.

Do you want to lose weight? Eat a piece of your favorite fruit instead of that hotdog. You might inspire yourself to also go for a walk.

Do you want to read more? Begin reading one page of a book, and before you realize it, you have read the first six pages.

Do you want to exercise more? On Mondays, Wednesdays, and Fridays, pack your gym bag with some clothes and go to the gym before or after work. You will soon be going to the gym without even thinking about it.

The most important factor here is to just start. That's the only way to create new habits. I'm not talking about the just doing something for the first time, but continuing to do it a consistent basis. This isn't about performance, it is more about consistently taking action. There is plenty of time to improve later on, just give yourself two minutes of uninterrupted effort.

This rule isn't about what you achieve, instead it is about the process of starting something. It is about training yourself into commencing without question. Knowing that two minutes is your minimum requirement, you don't feel overloaded by the thought of exerting hours on end. Your focus will be on taking the actions needed and allowing things to proceed from there.

Just Do It

I can't make any guarantees about whether or not this rule will work for you, but I can say for sure that it won't work if you don't try it.

The main problem with many things you read, listen to, or watch is that you may understand the process, but you don't ever begin practicing it. I want this chapter to be different for you. I want you to use this information right in this moment.

What is something that you can do right now that is going to take you under two minutes to do? Just do it now…

Anybody can spare just 120 seconds of their day. Use this time wisely and get something done. Get up and move. Go!

Do It Right

Now, there is one problem with the two-minute rule, and that is if it isn't used correctly, things can go slightly wrong.

Many people interpret this rule to mean that if you know you can do something in less than two minutes, just do it regardless. However, you need to apply this rule during processing time. This is the main factor that most people who follow this rule often forget to mention. If it is used at the wrong time, this rule could mistakenly derail your productivity. For instance, whilst reading this book you realize that could complete another task in two minutes and tick it off your list. However, this will interfere with your current reading. Can you see how that could be counter intuitive? I know I asked you this time, but keep this in mind.

Processing Time

Processing time is the time it takes you to figure out what actions you need to take to do things. Let's take a look at going through your email for example. For me, this means I have to look at each individual message and then figure out what actions I need to take, like moving it into my task list, filing it, or deleting it. It isn't important to start or finish a task that an email contains, whether it is a response or concluding a specific request. The processing time is purely the time used to organize and manage your future actions.

Purpose of The Two Minute Rule

The main benefit of this practice is that it helps you swiftly tick off items on your to-do list. When you can see a task that can be completed fast, and you take the action needed, you can stop "planning" the task, "dreading" the task, and thinking about the task. You just quickly complete the task, and move on. We are training our brains toward a "bias for action."

By taking actions on the information in front of us, we can stop things from accumulating around us. These actions can help us eliminate the clutter in our lives. Without all the clutter and distractive thoughts you can be less inclined to procrastinate and improve your productivity. Ticking a few simple items off your list can be highly rewarding and drive you to keep on ticking off boxes. Use this to your advantage and roll with it.

Why You Shouldn't Use This Rule When any Task Pops Into Your Head

This is when the two-minute rule can derail your productivity. Other than being used during your processing time, the two-minute rule has to be related to what you are doing right at that moment.

Take the email example from above. Let's imagine that you open an email that may only take you two minutes to respond, rather than leaving it, you take the action needed to complete it. Your goal was "processing your email," so responding to one will help you with your goal, right?

Here is instance of what may transpire:

You sit down at your desk and realize that you have some important messages that you haven't handled yet. You decide to spend an hour working on processing your inbox.

You look at the first message, but a thought pops into your mind that isn't related like: "Oh, I need to run some errands after work, so I need to set a reminder about this in my calendar so I don't forget. Putting that on my calendar will take me less than two minutes, so I need to do it now, and get it out of the way."

So, you decide to minimize your email application and open up your calendar and add the errand in for 6pm. But then you begin thinking: "Wait a minute, the weatherman gave out rain for this evening, let me check." Since this, too will only take two minutes. You pull out your phone and open the weather app, you immediately see: "Deadly tornado rips through Oklahoma."

You realize you have family in Oklahoma so you watch the video to find out where the tornado touched down and to see if there are any causalities. Once the video ends and you see that thankfully, none of your relatives were involved.

You put away your phone, and your stomach growls, so you decide to take a break and get something to eat. You walk down the street to the coffee stand and grab a cup of coffee and a bagel. On the way back to your office, a coworker bumps into you and asks if you have a minute.

You think: "I can't be rude, it will only take a minute." The conversation took longer than a minute, and you find yourself in deep conversation.

Around one hour later, you finally sit back down at your desk. You maximize your email back to full screen, and you see that you have received an additional 20 new messages. You had two other projects that you were supposed to work on today, and you haven't begun either one of them. To make the situation worse, your boss asks everyone to gather for a meeting.

Your goal when you sat down two hours ago was to get your email processed. You didn't process ANY emails, and you gained 20 additional messages. You have made minimal to no progress, and are a further two hours short of time than you started with.

Does this sound familiar?

If you use the two-minute rule at any time of the day, you will just be going from task to task all day long, running from thought to thought rather than proceeding in a logical and productive manner.

If you use the two-minute rule every time a two-minute task pops into our heads, our intentions and plans will be repetitively derailed.

Anytime I am faced with a huge project, my mind has this innate ability to come up with all sorts of two minutes tasks that keep me derailed all day long. Rather than being bias for action, this rule has become a tool to help us procrastinate. Once you realize this, you can shift your perspective and use it to your advantage during certain times.

Chapter Six:

Mindset Hacking

Everyone wants more out of life. Most people find themselves chasing love, success, happiness, or money. We might not want to admit it, but it is true in some shape or form.

Everybody that wants to increase their income will look for new jobs that pay more, work longer hours or attempt to open their own business. They may try to improve or increase their marketing strategies, go to multiple networking events or study to add to their qualifications. The list can go on and on.

When you are looking for love, you might decide to join a dating app. If you are already in a relationship, you might schedule some date nights in effort to spend more time with a desirable partner. Some people might resort to developing affairs trying to find the love they crave.

To get healthier, you might hire a personal trainer. You want to lose weight so you switch up your eating habits and find all the information you can on the latest fad diet.

Every one of these desires force us to perform changed behaviors.

The Hack to Bring You More

This mindset hack is so simple that you might not believe me. If you would like to have more in your life, that secret to this is learning to accept compliments.

Yes, you did read that right. Once you can start accepting compliments, you will increase your ability for success, experience more happiness, and earn more money. Hang in there and let me explain.

Imagine that today is a normal day. It isn't a holiday, your birthday, or any day that you expect a gift or compliment. It is just a normal, ordinary day. You meet your best friend for lunch, and out of the blue, they give you a compliment, or they buy your lunch.

How would you react? If you are like most people, you might say something like: "Oh, you shouldn't have done that." or "Next time it's on me." They might compliment your outfit, and you react with "This old thing?" If you react in this way, you are unconsciously and actively REJECTING their gift or compliment.

In this day and time, when anyone gives us a compliment or buys us a gift it kicks us out of having total control. If we sit back and receive these gifts, we aren't in control. Just think about it for a minute, who has control of the compliment or gift? The person giving it. Who has control over an intention? The person giving it. They are also in control of when and how they present it to us.

We are merely in control of our own response or reaction. From an evolutionary and primal standpoint, where we aren't in control, we become vulnerable, we feel exposed, and potentially at a disadvantage. In order to regain control, we will usually give them a compliment or a gift in return, or alternatively completely reject it.

The Problem

The main problem with this kind of societal and primal patterning is that it creates a belief in our unconscious mind that it isn't safe to receive these offerings. Our unconscious mind is very suggestive and totally illogical, and loves to make associations, such as connecting behaviors and beliefs that we normally would not logically or consciously associate with each other.

If we make suggestions to our unconscious mind that it isn't safe to receive small offerings such as gifts or compliments, our unconscious mind will expand on this manner of thinking and apply these thoughts to receiving any reward. To our unconscious mind, if a small gift isn't safe to receive, then what makes accepting a lot of money from a client safe?

Since our brains are very symbolic, it believes that receiving anything is somewhat the same. These beliefs extend a lot farther than just obtaining monetary benefits. It can impact our ability to generate income, revenue, or even accepting things as simple as new opportunities, new clients, or referrals to expand our businesses to new heights.

If you have a goal of growing your business or income, you might need to implement new strategies like creating referral partnerships or pushing ads on social media. These activities could prove to be fruitless if you have wired your brain to not acknowledge any leads that you might generate.

If you want to welcome more adoration from your significant other, it won't matter what they might do to demonstrate more love. You are never going to feel or appreciate the affection that they have been giving you since you have trained yourself to block any loving praises. This applies to your life in general, and also your health. You have told your unconscious mind's filtering system that it isn't safe to receive. This means that you may not be able to appreciate any new opportunities to their fullest potential.

The next time somebody offers you a compliment or presents you a small gift out of nowhere, graciously accept it and simply say: "thank you so much." Do this every single time somebody wants to gift you anything, and do not reject or welcome any negative thinking. In order to rewire your brain, it is going to take repetition. It won't be enough to accept just one compliment, you will just go back to your old habits. Start implementing this behavior of accepting gifts right now and consistently, and you will begin seeing changes in your life immediately.

Chapter Seven:

Healthy Habits for Discipline

Considering the fact that most of what we do every day is habit-driven, developing healthy habits will instill the right amount of discipline into your life. The following habits will help make self-discipline easier to implement. Remember that all habits will take time to form and break. If you start out small and build from there, you won't be wondering how to find discipline since you will embody the habits you need to acquire it.

Forgiveness

This probably doesn't even sound like a habit, and that's because most people live their life without ever forgiving people for any wrongdoings. We live a large portion of our lives in a state of guilt, regret, or anger, and this is only going to cause more problems. Anger and hate consume a lot more energy than forgiveness and love. When you forgive, you learn to let go of things that aren't serving you.

Without making forgiveness a habit, you won't be able to find your self-discipline. You will be too worried about how somebody has wronged you to focus on your goals. Forgiving them doesn't mean that you forget what they did, or that you will welcome them back into your life. It simply means you are releasing the negative energy they created in your life.

Meditation

Meditation offers you some time to put your mind at ease. It grounds and bestows you with a place to cultivate and grow. When you meditate, you cancel out the noise and realize that you're just one of many connected to the universe.

Meditation also has a huge impact on your self-discipline. It helps to clear the mind and sets up the tone for the day. It improves your mental, spiritual, emotional, and physical health, which allows you to reap some of the biggest results for minimal time invested.

You can meditate in just ten minutes or for as long as you'd like. All you have to do is keep the mind still, and if it does start to wander, just reel it back it in. Meditation is all about aligning the physical body with the spiritual body. Once they are aligned, you can live a more focused life. I would highly recommend guided mediation for beginners, you can find an abundance of videos and walkthroughs on YouTube if you need.

Try A Dopamine Fast

This isn't something you need to do regularly, but it can be helpful if you feel like you need a mental reset, even just once to expand your perspective. Dopamine is a chemical release within your body that plays a part in how you feel pleasure. Dopamine is linked with the bodies reward system. Every time you scroll through Instagram, watch something on Netflix, receive a like on Facebook, eat a burger, play a video game, or masturbate, your brain receives a hit of dopamine.

The brain is addicted to dopamine, as it is what makes us happy. The brain will try to stimulate the repetition of behaviors that produce dopamine, and that's where things can go bad. Don't get me wrong, dopamine isn't something wicked or evil. It is a complex neurochemical that is responsible for motivation, decision making, and attention. There is no need to fear dopamine at all, it's the fact that there are man-made pleasures that abuse dopamine in unnatural ways that cause the problem. This is how people become addicted to things like alcohol, drugs, and food. Excluding substances, screens or any other stimuli, you may become reacquainted with yourself.

Dopamine fasting is not about changing the dopamine system in your brain. Instead, fasting offers you the time and atmosphere to reflect on the origins and causes of your addictive behaviors. If this is something of interest to you, you can try out 24-hour dopamine fast. The rules of a dopamine fast are as follows. Try not to perform any of the following activities for 24-hours:

- No electronics
- No reading magazines or books
- No masturbation or sex
- No podcasts or music
- No coffee or any other type of stimulants
- No food

There are things that you can do, you just have to get creative. Some examples are:

- Drink water
- Visualize
- Deep thinking
- Exercise
- Meditate
- Journal

This may seem strict, and it is, but it is only for 24-hours, and a good portion of that you will be sleeping. If you can't achieve this for only 24 hours, then you know how serious your addictions are. While we just accept the fact that we are slaves to our phones, TV, computer, and so on, it's unhealthy.

You may find that during those 24-hours, you are able to push through something that you had been struggling with for some time. As I said, this works like a mental reset. It will remove you from a fast-paced distraction-overloaded world so that you will be able to focus on what is important.

It will bring awareness to your dopamine cravings and where you tend to make undisciplined decisions. With this awareness, you will be able to override your inner resistance in the future. Sit in silence, meditate, journal/reflect on some revealing questions you might have for yourself. Approach the fast with the intention of mapping out and reflecting on your behaviors.

During this fast, boredom will surely strike. You have to embrace this boredom and understand that this boredom is where normally you would fall back on your addiction. You will find other things to do, this is only temporary.

Persistence

Of course, no habit is going to stick unless you have persistence. Persistence is what helps you to not give up. Even when you do slip up, it gives you the chance to get back up again. Without persistence, self-discipline would be impossible.

Why? Because reaching any sort of goal is difficult. It is easy to get discouraged and quitting takes a lot less energy and effort than pushing through, especially when something inflicts a lot of pain before you reach the pleasure.

But that's what it takes. What you have to realize is that even the most famous people out there that seem to succeed at everything have failed many times. Failure is important. Without failing, you won't be able to achieve your greatest goals.

There are many ways to instill this habit, but the best is to come up with a profound reason why you want the things in life that you do. Once you have strong enough motives, they can help push you through just about anything.

Chapter Eight:

Navy Seals to The Rescue

The Navy Seals are the US Navy's principal special operations force. Their job is mentally, physically, and emotionally demanding. Most people who try out to be a Seal don't make it through the vigorous protocols. What separates those who do from those who get sent home is their mental fortitude.

We're going to look at some Navy Seal mindset-hacks that will help you become mentally resilient, and how you can focus them toward your goals.

Up The Ante

Chad Williams, a Navy Seal, explains that when you are laboring toward a goal, you should work to 'up the ante' so that you continue to move forward until you have reached success. Consistently ask yourself, "What's at stake?"

The higher your purse, the greater the odds are that you will persevere. That means, the more you up the ante, the more mental fortitude you will have. Let's say you want to run a 10K. In order to hold yourself accountable, you give your friend $50 and tell them that they can only give it back to you once you have completed the 10K. There is a good chance that you will quit before you reach that goal.

Why? A 10K requires a lot of training and dedication, and that $50 is quickly going to not be that big of a deal when you start gasping for air, your calves tense up, your heel starts blistering and you just don't have much left in the tank. Now obviously giving your friend $500 might make it more motivating, and you may be more reluctant to give up so easily. However, it's not overly sustainable to rely on your friend every time you need to do a hard task, right? But, what happens if you change the stake?

- When I train for a 10K, I will lose 20 pounds. This will make me healthier, I'll look better, and I will find it easier to get around.

- If I do run a 10K, it will show my children that they can do anything they set their mind to.

- Developing the discipline to run a 10K will help me to reach all of my other goals.

Once you have a higher stake, there is a greater chance that you will stick with it. Something that Williams does is trick himself into believing that everything is on the line. He goes so far as to tell himself that if he doesn't reach his goal, his family will die. Most people aren't going to go that far, but you can still take things to the worst-case scenario to help motivate yourself to push through if that's what you need.

It may seem drastic, but when you trick your mind into thinking that the stakes are high, you're more likely to persevere.

Bounce Back Fast

There are a lot of Navy Seals books out there outlining the training they had to go through, and how they developed their mental fortitude, enabling them to endure through many life-threatening situations. Something that most of the Seals mention is bouncing back quickly after something unexpected occurs.

Before heading out on a mission, the Navy Seals are briefed on what they may face and what to expect. For example, if they are getting ready to rescue somebody from a hijacked ship, they will be briefed on information like:

- The ship's layout.
- How many people are on board.
- The types of weapons they might encounter.
- How to move through the ship undetected.
- Who the target may be.

However, most of the time, things aren't going to go as planned. They may get on the ship and come across an obstacle that wasn't in the plans. What are they supposed to do? They certainly aren't going to stop to figure out who is to blame for not telling them about the hindrance, neither are they going to just give up and return back to home base.

The ability to adapt and move forward regardless of any adversity or obstacle in the way is what makes these Seals outstanding. To be mentally tough, you have to learn how to bounce back when you face something that you did not expect. Trick the brain into overcoming that need to argue about what is happening. When something comes up, figure it out and move forward. Repeat this phrase to yourself, "Acknowledge, accept, adapt, act."

Visualize

During training, Seals are taught to visualize themselves successfully completing their mission. They are training and preparing their mind for what they are getting ready to do. Envisioning as many outcomes as possible helps the Seals to mentally prepare for any situation.

No matter what your goal may be, visualize yourself pushing through, working through obstacles, shutting out that inner critic, and ignoring anybody who says you can't. If you "see" yourself working through those hurdles before you start, when you actually reach them, your mind won't have to figure out what to do. You will already know how to keep going.

Recite a Mantra

Former Navy Seal Richard Machowicz wrote in his book *'Unleash the Warrior Within'* that he received a picture from a friend. In the photo was his friend's brother, another Navy Seal, and many other Seals who were all getting ready to jump from a plane.

On the back, there was a quote that said, "A man can be beaten in two ways: if he gives up or he dies." Mack took this quote and came up with the mantra, "Not dead, can't quit."

He would recite that during his training, and he believes that this mantra was what helped him become a Navy Seal. You'll find it's easier to be mentally tough when your mind works in favor of the toughness and not against it. That's why it helps to recite a mantra, whether you use Mack's or create your own. Some other options for mantras are:

- Quitting is not an option.

- Now or never.

If somebody is driving you to quit, or the voice in your head becomes negative, say your mantra. Trick the brain into believing that the only option you have is to keep going.

One of the most important parts of getting what you want from life is to be mentally tough. Apply these mindset hacks, and you will develop the mental toughness that you will need to reach your goals.

Chapter Nine:

Popular Self-Discipline Tactics

With everything we have discussed so far, you should have a pretty good idea of how to improve your self-discipline. That's not going to stop us from providing you with a few more tactics for busting through those bad habits and taking control of your life.

The fact of the matter is, it doesn't matter what kind of day planner or time management app you use. There are millions of ways to keep track of and measure your habits, but they aren't going to work unless you can make them stick. What it boils down to is that self-discipline is a state of mind, not an app.

Before we go over some more specific ways to improve your self-discipline, answer this question, what do you want to achieve? You're reading this book for a reason, so there has to be something that you are looking to achieve that you believe self-discipline will help you with. If you don't have a goal, then it is going to be way too easy to just give up when things get tough.

You need to make sure that your desire for your goal is stronger than the temptation to give up, so figure out what it is that you really want. Do you want to be more productive so that you have more time to spend with your family? Would you like to create healthy exercise and eating habits so that you feel more confident? Have you always wanted to launch your own freelance career so that you can work wherever you want?

The motivation to achieve self-discipline must come from within you. It's not going to last if you are doing it just because you think it is something that you should do. With that in mind, here are the last self-discipline strategies, concepts, and mindset shifts that can help you.

Keep in mind, there is no need to use every single one of these as they may not be relevant to your situation. Realistically, applying a couple of these strategies should give you a fundamental shift in your self-discipline capacity.

Challenge Your Excuses

One of my friends used to say that she didn't have enough time to start her personal blog because she had a full-time job as a financial consultant. After working on things for her clients all day, she was too tired to sit at her computer, and didn't want to take the time to work on her writing.

One day, I spoke up and said that if she continued to make excuses, that she would never have the time to build toward her dream. She took some time to respond to me after this, but is forever grateful that I challenged her thinking. Now she takes 30 minutes before work to write for her beauty blog first thing in the morning so she cannot make any excuses. While 30 minutes might not sound like a lot, it adds up over time.

Try giving this a shot with your own excuses. If you are thinking, "I can't eat healthy because I don't have the time to fix my diet," try preparing a large batch of healthy food on a day when you aren't that busy. If you say, "I can't write a book because I work full time," try working on your book for an hour each evening instead of watching TV. There is always time, it's about choosing what is more important to you. What are your priorities? Do you want to watch TV and never write that book you have always dreamed of writing? That's fine. But if there is anything worse than failing, it's the regret you later feel, knowing that you never tried.

Delay Gratification

To build up your self-discipline, you have to know how to avoid temptation so that you can hold out for things that are better. There have been studies that have shown that delaying gratification is an important trait in successful individuals.

Sigmund Freud explained that as a child, we are all focused on receiving immediate gratification. As we get older, we start to tolerate discomfort at various levels to realize bigger goals.

For example, if you stop going out every weekend with your friends, you can save money to buy a home or travel abroad. You could resist the urge to eat the donuts in the break room in order to enjoy the health benefits of a better diet. When we make the choice to delay gratification, we are looking out for our future selves.

Consistent Small Habits

Brad Isaac, back when he was budding comedian, asked Jerry Seinfeld for advice. Seinfeld said that in order to become a better comedian, he should work on his jokes every day. He said, get a red marker and a large wall calendar, and for each day that he wrote a new joke, he was to mark off the day with a big red X.

After some time, you are going to start building up a chain of red X's. That's going to feel very satisfying, and that sensation should drive you to make sure that chain doesn't break.

Focus less on achieving amazing results initially, and more about building a consistent habit. After you feel this practice is settling into your routine, you will start to see remarkable results. It is important that you choose a task that is significant enough to make a difference, but is also simple enough that you can easily practice it each day without question.

Nutrition, Sleep, and Exercise

If you haven't been getting enough sleep, eating well, and exercising, and you are trying to improve your self-discipline, you're fighting an uphill battle. When you take care of yourself and your body, you are going to find it a lot easier to work towards your goals. You will find that you have more energy, a better attitude, and you will be less likely to quit when things get tough.

Unfortunately, sleep is often overlooked by many individuals as the cause of many of their problems. To check if your sleeping pattern is something you could remedy you could monitor your sleep cycle, and refine it to a more optimal level. A great free application to track your sleep is Sleep Cycle – Sleep Tracker by Sleep Cycle AB, but there are many more on the app store. This app will enable you to track your sleep quality, regularity and even detect snoring or sleep talking.

Before bed encourage yourself to follow a night time routine that helps you wind down. 30 minutes before bed you may choose to partake in some stretching, reading, meditation, journaling, breathwork or even a combination of a few.

It's The Habit, Not the Result

Instead of claiming, "I want to lose weight" try, "I want to walk 10,000 steps a day." The idea of losing weight is hard to pin down. How can you achieve it, and how can you track your success?

It is a lot easier to track the concrete goal of walking 10,000 steps each day. If you stay focused on reaching that habit, losing weight is likely going to come with it. Figure out what it is that you would like to achieve and then figure out what habit is going to help your reach that goal.

Tony Robbins once said "It's not about achieving the goal. It's about who you have to become in order to achieve the goal. The juice in in the growth."

You Can't Improve Things That Aren't Measured

There is a chance that you have heard this saying, but it's true. Measuring your progress is one of the most powerful ways to motivate yourself to do better. When you clearly track things that you find important, it is going to help you to better understand how you perform, and you can improve.

Everything you want to improve can be measured, from minutes spent exercising to how many books you read a year. You can use a device or an application, or you can track your progress using a notebook or spreadsheet. How you measure your success doesn't matter; it is the act of measuring that is going to help you succeed.

For example, a budget app will help you to keep track of your financials, incoming and outgoing. Seeing the amount of money you spend on late-night burritos or online shopping can encourage you to make some changes to these habits. When you watch your savings go up every month, it will keep you motivated to maintain better financial decisions. While calculating your progress, remember that the only person you are measuring against is your past self, not anybody else.

Eat The Frog

This is probably one of the most popular self-discipline tactics, and it comes to us from Mark Twain. He said, "If it's your job to eat a frog, it's best to do it first thing in the morning. If it's your job to eat two frogs, it's best to eat the biggest one first."

That frog is a big, daunting task you need to complete but are likely to avoid. In taking care of that task first thing, you will begin with a clear mind, heightened willpower, complete concentration and full of energy. If you end up pushing it back toward the end of the day, you will most likely end up too tired, and probably say something like, "I'll do it tomorrow."

In order to eat the frog, come up with a to-do list the night before and put the hardest, biggest, ugliest task at the very beginning of the list. When you start working, take action right away and don't move onto anything else on your list until you have finished "eating the frog."

Once you have finished that task, you will feel a sense of relief and fulfilment because the hardest part of your day is complete, and rest of your to-do list is going to be much easier in comparison.

You Don't Have to Get Permission

If you are waiting to receive approval from somebody, don't. Cultivating self-discipline means that you can find approval within yourself. There are a lot of us who hold back on working toward our goals because we are afraid that others will think it's weird, crazy or outlandish. After you release that need for approval, you are free to follow your goals and work on the things that are most important.

Additionally, liberation from yourself is incredibly important. Stop the negative self-talk and forget what you or anyone else thinks. You need to free yourself of this way of thinking and take action! You are worthy, you are smart enough, you are absolutely capable.

Have A Support System

You might not need the permission or approval of others to work toward your goals, but you do need to have some form of support system. You should not isolate yourself. Having a group of people who believe in you, provides you with incredible value when it comes to working toward a difficult goal.

It's important to make sure you are surrounded by people who want to see you succeed. This can be hard sometimes because there are family and friends who will say destructive and mean things out of envy or jealousy. Some may even tell you that you shouldn't try to reach those goals, or say that your goals are silly, impossible, or pointless.

Ignore those people; they are only looking out for themselves and trying to justify their own insecurities. Instead, find those who want to see you succeed and are happy for you when you reach the goals you have set for yourself, even the small wins. Avoiding toxic people whether they are family or not is a crucial step you may need to consider to truly feel at peace. Take some time away and focus on yourself for a little bit.

Budget Energy, Not Time

What time of the day do you feel more focused? Everybody has a different circadian rhythm. Some people focus better first thing in the morning, and then there are some who have more energy at night. It doesn't matter which category you fall into. Neither is right or wrong. The important thing is to work around the times when you naturally have the most energy.

Of course, having a full-time job makes this a bit harder to do since you can't really choose what hours you work, but you could still use this information to help you make decisions. For example, whether you go to the gym before or after work.

Don't Expect To Be Perfect

Don't expect yourself to be perfect in everything you do. If you are holding yourself to a standard that nobody can achieve, you will succeed at nothing, making yourself feel horrible and inadequate in the process. Remember this quote, "Don't be afraid to start over. This time you're not starting from scratch, you're starting from experience." To me this quote sums it up perfectly. Shift your perspective into converting your failures into lessons. You didn't fail, you learnt. Now you are one step closer to succeeding.

When you fail, and it will happen, forgive yourself, and move forward. You could end up missing a workout, and that's fine, but you know that the next day you're going to make up for it.

Slipping up does not make you a failure. All it means is that you are human. Making sure that you improve your self-discipline isn't about not making any mistakes. It's about the determination and grit you have to keep pushing forward and improving yourself over a long term stretch.

Self-discipline is like any other muscle in your body. It won't explode overnight, but it will grow over time with consistent, hard work.

There is no need to try and master your self-discipline in a single day. The important thing is to start implementing a single one of these strategies and then take incremental steps toward growing that muscle.

Conclusion

Deciding to grow your self-discipline and change your life for the better is not an easy task. It will require making changes and a deep and personal conversation with yourself about what you really want in life. The important thing is to make sure that you figure out what works for you. Some of the tricks we have gone over may not work well or at all, and others will work like a charm. Don't think just because your friend has seen success with a certain method, that you will too.

The main thing you need to make sure that you do is start writing in a journal and come up with goals and ambitions to work toward. That way you will know exactly what you want and what you need to do to get there. Without that information, you will struggle to define a pathway and improve your self-discipline because you won't know where to start.

Figure out how you will hold yourself accountable and stick to your goals. Stay consistent in all that you do, and stay strong. Once you find what works, double down on that. Above all else, don't give up. Continue pushing until you find your key to success!

Finally, if you found this book useful in any way, a review on Amazon would be sincerely appreciated!

www.ingramcontent.com/pod-product-compliance
Lightning Source LLC
Chambersburg PA
CBHW071757080526
44588CB00013B/2278